Made in America in a I
on hydro-generated po
has long been a favorite of knitters and crocheters.
Lovely, lofty and quick to knit or crochet, Homespun
is available in dozens of beautifully blended colorways,
from heathery tweeds to painterly palettes and makes
even the simplest of projects look absolutely stunning.
Homespun's bulky weight results in a fast finish for
sweaters and afghans and its wash-and-wear care
makes it ideal for almost any project.

About Lion Brand® Yarn Company

Lion Brand Yarn Company is America's oldest hand knitting yarn brand.
Founded in 1878, Lion Brand Yarn Company is a leading supplier of quality
hand knitting and crochet yarns. Throughout its history, Lion Brand Yarn
has been at the forefront of yarn trends while consistently providing its
customers with the highest quality product at a value price. The company's
mission is to provide ideas, inspiration and education to yarn crafters.

LIBRARY CAPELET

◖■■☐◗ EASY +

SIZE
About 23 x 40 in. (58.5 x 101.5 cm)

MATERIALS
LION BRAND® HOMESPUN®
  #381 Barley 2 skeins
  or color of your choice
LION BRAND large-eyed blunt needle

ADDITIONAL MATERIALS
Circular knitting needle size 10 (6 mm) 29 in. (73.5 cm)
1 button 1 1/4 in. (32 mm) in diameter.

GAUGE
14 sts + 12 rows = 4 in. (10 cm) in St st (k on RS, p on WS).
BE SURE TO CHECK YOUR GAUGE.

> **TIP**
> Circular needles are often not marked for size
> and they almost always get separated from their
> original packages. Mark them with a fine-point
> permanent marker (two dots for size 2). The
> larger needles usually have enough space to mark
> the actual number. It works for all needles —
> wood, metal, and plastic.

STITCH PATTERNS
K1, p1 Rib

Row 1 (RS): K1, p1 across.

Row 2: K the knit sts and p the purl sts.
Rep Row 2 for K1, p1 Rib.

Seed Stitch (over an even number of sts)
Row 1 (RS): *K1, p1; rep from * across.

Row 2: P the knit sts and k the purl sts.
Rep Row 2 for Seed st.

NOTES
1) Circular needle is used to accommodate large number of sts. Work back and forth on circular needle as if working on straight needles.
2) To keep Collar folded down, button Capelet through both buttonholes.

CAPELET
Body
Cast on 160 sts.
Work in Seed St until piece measures 2½ in. (6.5 cm) from beg.
Beg with a k row, work in St st (k on RS, p on WS) for 4 rows.

Next Row: (K18, k2tog) across – 8 sts dec.
Work even in St st for 3 rows.

Next Row: (k17, k2tog) across.
Continue as established, working in St st and dec
8 sts every 4 rows, until only 8 sts remain. Bind off.

Collar
With RS facing, beg at top right corner, pick up and k 100 sts
evenly spaced along straight edge of Body.

Rows 1-5: Work in Seed st.

Row 6 (Buttonhole row): Work 4 sts in Seed st, k2tog,
yo, work even in Seed st to end.

Rows 7-13: Work in Seed st.

Row 14 (Buttonhole row): Rep Row 6.

Rows 15-20: Work in Seed St. Bind off.

FINISHING
Fold Collar in half, so that last buttonhole is directly over
the first. Sew button opposite buttonhole. Button through
both or just one buttonhole. Weave in ends.

SHADED TRIANGLES WRAP

The Shaded Triangle Wrap is made using directional knitting to create triangular shading across the Wrap.

■■■□□ EASY +

SIZE
About 18 x 86 in. (46 x 218.5 cm)

MATERIALS
LION BRAND® HOMESPUN®
   #315 Tudor 3 skeins
   or color of your choice
LION BRAND knitting needles size 11 (8 mm)
LION BRAND crochet hook size K-10.5 (6.5 mm)
LION BRAND large-eyed blunt needle

GAUGE
EXACT GAUGE IS NOT ESSENTIAL TO THIS PROJECT.

NOTES
1) Knitting begins with a triangle shape, then stitches are picked up and six more triangles are worked to make this rectangular wrap.
2) Take care to turn work at the end of a triangle only when instructed to do so.

WRAP
First Triangle
Cast on 47 sts.

Rows 1 and 2: Sl 1, k to end of row.

Rows 3 and 4: Sl 1, k to last 2 sts, k2tog – 46 sts. Repeat Rows 1-4 until 3 sts remain.

Next Row: Sl 1, k2tog, pass slipped stitch over; do not turn work.

Second Triangle
Working along left edge of triangle just completed, pick up and knit 46 sts (for a total of 47 sts). Work as for First Triangle, beg with Row 2.

Third Triangle
Work as for Second Triangle. Turn work.

Fourth-Seventh Triangles
Work as for Second and Third Triangles.

FINISHING
Edging
From right side, with crochet hook, join yarn with sl st in edge of Wrap. Work sc evenly around outside edge of Wrap; join with sl st in first sc. Fasten off.

> **TIP**
>
> Yarn storage can be a challenge! To keep unruly skeins under control, take an old pair of nylon stockings and cut them into 4"-6" tubes. Stretch the tubes over your skeins and they won't unravel. This is especially handy when you have several colors of yarn in your knitting bag.

PERFECT POCKETED SHAWL

Shown on page 11.

 EASY +

SIZE
About 9 x 58 in. (23 x 147.5 cm)

MATERIALS
LION BRAND® HOMESPUN®
   #322 Baroque 2 skeins (A)
   #411 Mixed Berries 1 skein (B)
   or colors of your choice
LION BRAND crochet hook size N-13 (9 mm)
LION BRAND large-eyed blunt needle

GAUGE
8 sts + 9 rows = 4 in. (10 cm) in sc.
8 sts + 6 rows = 4 in. (10 cm) in (sc, dc) pattern.
BE SURE TO CHECK YOUR GAUGE.

STITCH EXPLANATIONS

FPDC (front post double crochet) Yarn over, insert hook from front to back then to front again, around post of st, draw up a loop, (yarn over and draw through 2 loops on hook) twice.

BPDC (back post double crochet) Yarn over, insert hook from back to front then to back again, around post of st, draw up a loop, (yarn over and draw through 2 loops on hook) twice.

sc2tog (sc decrease) Insert hook into st and draw up a loop. Insert hook into next st and draw up a loop. Yarn over, draw through all 3 loops on hook.

SHAWL

With A, ch 19.

Row 1: Sc in 2nd ch from hook and in each ch across – 18 sc.

Row 2: Ch 1, turn, sc in first 2 sts, ch 3, (sc in next 2 sts, ch 3) 7 times, sc in last 2 sts – 18 sc and 8 ch-3 loops.

Row 3: Ch 1, turn, sc in each sc across, skipping the ch-3 loops.

Row 4: Ch 1, turn, *sc in next st, dc in next st; rep from * across.
Rep last row until piece measures 68 in. (172.5 cm) from beginning.

Next 2 Rows: Ch 1, turn, sc in each st across.

Last 2 Rows: Rep Rows 2 and 3.
Fasten off.

Finishing
Fold short ends up 6 in. (15 cm) to form pockets, push ch-3 loops to right side. Pin in place.

Edging
From right side, beginning at top corner of one pocket, join B with sl st, *working through both thicknesses, work 13 sc along side of pocket to next corner, work 3 sc in corner, 16 sc along lower edge of pocket, 3 sc in next corner, 13 sc along side of pocket; work 89 sc along side of Shawl to top corner of second pocket; rep from * to finish second pocket and opposite side of Shawl; join with sl st in first sc. Do not fasten off.

Collar
Note: Collar is worked in rows across last 89 sts and with B only.

Row 1: Ch 1, turn, sc in first st, dc in next 87 sts, sc in last st – 89 sts.

Row 2: Ch 1, turn, sc2tog, *FPDC around next st, BPDC around next st; rep from * across to last 3 sts, FPDC around next st, sc2tog – 87 sts.

Row 3: Ch 1, turn, skip first st, sc2tog, *BPDC around next st, FPDC around next st; rep from * across to last 2 sts, sc2tog – 84 sts.

Row 4: Ch 1, turn, skip first st, sc2tog, *BPDC around next st, FPDC around next st; rep from * across to last 3 sts, BPDC around next st, sc2tog – 81 sts.

Row 5: Ch 1, turn, skip first st, sc2tog, *FPDC around next st, BPDC around next st; rep from * across to last 2 sts, sc2tog – 78 sts.

Row 6: Ch 1, turn, skip first sc, sc2tog, *FPDC around next st, BPDC around next st; rep from * across to last 3 sts, FPDC around next st, sc2tog – 75 sts.

Row 7: Rep Row 3 – 72 sts. Fasten off.

FINISHING
Weave in ends.

> It is always better to join a new ball of yarn at the beginning of a row, rather than in the middle. If you are worried that you are going to run out of yarn, measure it against your outstretched arm. If you have at least four arm-lengths of yarn left, you can safely go across the row. If you don't have enough yarn, better to cut it, leaving a four-inch tail and use the yarn later to sew up your sweater.

TIP

PAINTED SHAWL

■■■□□ EASY

SIZE
About 36 x 74 in. (91.5 x 188 cm) including edging

MATERIALS
LION BRAND® HOMESPUN®
> #408 Wildfire 4 skeins
> or color of your choice

LION BRAND crochet hook size N-13 (9 mm)
LION BRAND large-eyed blunt needle

GAUGE
8 sts + 8 rows = 4 in. (10 cm) in hdc.
BE SURE TO CHECK YOUR GAUGE.

SHAWL
Ch 4; join with sl st in first ch to form a ring.

Row 1 (RS): Ch 3 (counts as hdc, ch 1 here and throughout), 3 hdc in ring, ch 1, hdc in ring – 5 hdc and 2 ch-1 sp.

> **TIP**
>
> Thick yarns combined with a big hook make projects easy and quick to complete. Such yarn is ideal for shawls and other outerwear garments.

Row 2: Ch 3, turn, sk first ch-1 sp, 2 hdc in next hdc, hdc in next hdc, 2 hdc in next hdc, ch 1, hdc in 2nd ch of turning ch – 7 hdc and 2 ch-1 sp.

Row 3: Ch 3, turn, sk first ch-1 sp, 2 hdc in next hdc, hdc in next 3 hdc, 2 hdc in next hdc, ch 1, hdc in 2nd ch of turning ch – 9 hdc and 2 ch-1 sp.

Row 4: Ch 3, turn, sk first ch-1 sp, 2 hdc in next hdc, hdc in each hdc to last hdc before ch-1 sp, 2 hdc in next hdc, ch 1, hdc in 2nd ch of turning ch – 11 hdc and 2 ch-1 sp. Rep Row 4 until Shawl measures 35 in. (89 cm) from beginning. Fasten off.

FINISHING
Shell Edging
Note: Edging is worked along both side edges, from tip of Shawl to top edge. The edging sts are worked in the ends of every other row. Join yarn with sl st in beg ch-4 ring.

First Shell
Row 1: Sl st around end of next row, ch 3, sk next row, sl st around end of next row – 1 ch-3 sp.

Row 2: Ch 2, turn, 6 hdc in ch-3 sp, sl st in sl st at beg of side edge (where yarn was joined).

Row 3: Ch 2 (counts as hdc), turn, hdc in same st, (hdc in next st, 2 hdc in next st) 3 times, sk next row of Shawl, sl st around end of next row – 11 hdc in first shell.

Next Shell

Row 4: Ch 3, do not turn, sk next row, sl st around end of next row – 1 ch-3 sp.

Row 5: Ch 2, turn, 6 hdc in ch-3 sp, sl st around 10th hdc of previous shell.

Row 6: Ch 2 (counts as hdc), turn, hdc in same st, (hdc in next st, 2 hdc in next st) 3 times, sk next row of Shawl, sl st around end of next row. Rep Rows 4–6 along side edge to top. Fasten off.
Join yarn in beg ch-4 ring and rep edging along other side of Shawl.

Weave in ends.

SANTA FE WRAP

 EASY

SIZES
S-L (1-2X)

Finished Chest 40 (44) in. (101.5 (112) cm)

Finished Length 25 (28) in. (63.5 (71) cm)

Note: Pattern is written for smallest size with changes for larger size in parentheses. When only one number is given, it applies to both sizes. To follow pattern more easily, circle all numbers pertaining to your size before beginning.

MATERIALS
LION BRAND® HOMESPUN®
    #409 Bourbon 7 (8) skeins
    or color of your choice
LION BRAND crochet hook size N-13 (9 mm)
LION BRAND large-eyed blunt needle

GAUGE
7 hdc = 3 in. (7.5 cm)
BE SURE TO CHECK YOUR GAUGE.

BACK
Ch 59 (66).

Row 1: Hdc in 3rd ch from hook and in each ch across—57 (64) sts.

Row 2 (RS): Ch 2, turn, hdc in each st across.
Rep Row 2 until piece measures 25 (28) in. (63.5 (71) cm) from beg. Fasten off.

LEFT FRONT
Work as for Back until piece measures 16 (18) in. (40.5 (45.5) cm) from beg.

Shape neck
Next Row (RS): Ch 2, turn, hdc in each st across to last 6 sts, leave remaining sts unworked – 51 (58) sts.

Next Row: Ch 2, turn, hdc in each st across.
Rep last 2 rows twice—39 (46) sts.
Rep last row until piece measures 25 (28) in. (63.5 (71) cm) from beg. Fasten off.

RIGHT FRONT
Work as for Left Front, reversing neck shaping.

FINISHING
Seam shoulders.

Edging
With RS facing, join yarn with sl st at a shoulder seam.

Rnds 1 and 2: Ch 1, sc evenly spaced around entire piece; join with sl st in first st.

Rnd 3: Ch 1, reverse sc (sc worked from left to right) in each st around. Fasten off.
Weave in ends.

THE BELLE SCARF

Shown on page 23.

Shown on page 23.

◧□□□ BEGINNER

SIZE
About 4 x 65 in. (10 x 165 cm)

MATERIALS
LION BRAND® HOMESPUN®
   #407 Painted Desert 1 skein
   or color of your choice
LION BRAND crochet hook size K-10.5 (6.5 mm)
LION BRAND large-eyed blunt needle

GAUGE
12 double crochet + 4 rows = 4 in. (10 cm).
BE SURE TO CHECK YOUR GAUGE.

TIP

Make a scrapbook of your knit or crochet projects by using a notebook, scrapbook, or binder. Begin by attaching your gauge swatch, a copy of the pattern, and an extra button on each page. Write down your needle or hook size, experiences you had while making it and for whom it was made. Include dates you started and finished and don't forget to include a photograph of you or someone you love with the finished project.

SCARF
Chain 140.

Row 1: Double crochet in 4th chain from hook, *double crochet in next chain, 2 double crochet in next chain; repeat from * across.

Row 2: Chain 3, turn, double crochet in same space, *double crochet in next 2 double crochet, 2 double crochet in next double crochet; repeat from * across.

Row 3: Chain 3, turn, double crochet in same space, *double crochet in next 3 double crochet, 2 double crochet in next double crochet; repeat from * across.

Row 4: Chain 3, turn, double crochet in same space, *double crochet in next 4 double crochet, 2 double crochet in next double crochet; repeat from * across.
Fasten off.

FINISHING
Weave in ends.

GENERAL INSTRUCTIONS

ABBREVIATIONS

beg = begin(ning)
BPDC = Back Post double crochet(s)
ch = chain
ch-sp = space previously made
cm = centimeters
dec = decreas(e)(s)(ing)
dc = double crochet
FPDC = Front Post double crochet(s)
hdc = half double crochet
k = knit
k2tog = knit 2 together
p = purl
mm = millimeters
rep = repeat(s)(ing
rnd(s) = round(s)
RS = right side
sc = single crochet
sk = skip
sl = slip
sl st = slip stitch
sp(s) = space(s)
st(s) = stitch(es)
St st = Stockinette stitch
tog = together
tr = treble (triple) crochet
WS = wrong side
yo = yarn over

* — When you see an asterisk used within a pattern row, the symbol indicates that later you will be told to repeat a portion of the instruction. Most often the instructions will say, repeat from * so many times.

( ) or [ ] — Set off a short number of stitches that are repeated or indicated additional information.

GAUGE

Never underestimate the importance of gauge. Achieving the correct gauge assures that the finished size of your piece matches the finished size given in the pattern.

CHECKING YOUR GAUGE

Work a swatch that is at least 4" (10 cm) square. Use the suggested needle or hook size and the number of stitches given. If your swatch is larger than 4" (10 cm), you need to work it again using a smaller hook; if it is smaller than 4" (10 cm), try it with a larger hook. The same concept applies if you are knitting. If your swatch is larger, work it again with smaller needles. If your swatch is larger, try smaller needles. This might require a swatch or two to get the exact gauge given in the pattern.

METRICS

As a handy reference, keep in mind that 1 ounce = approximately 28 grams and 1" = 2.5 centimeters.

TERMS

continue in this way or as established — Once a pattern is set up (established), the instructions may tell you to continue in the same way.

fasten off — To end your piece, you need to simply pull the yarn through the last loop left on the hook. This keeps the last stitch intact and prevents the work from unraveling.

right side — Refers to the front of the piece.

work even — This is used to indicate an area worked as established without increasing or decreasing.

POST STITCH

Work around post of stitch indicated, inserting hook in direction of arrow (Fig. 1).

Fig. 1

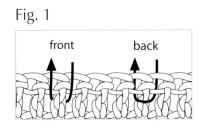

KNIT 2 TOGETHER (abbreviated k2tog)

Insert the right needle into the front of the first two stitches on the left needle as if to knit (Fig. 2), then knit them together as if they were one stitch.

Fig. 2

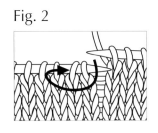

YARN OVER (abbreviated yo)

After a knit stitch, before a knit stitch
Bring the yarn forward between the needles, then back over the top of the right hand needle, so that it is now in position to knit the next stitch (Fig. 3a).

After a purl stitch, before a purl stitch
Take yarn over the right hand needle to the back, then forward under it, so that it is now in position to purl the next stitch (Fig. 3b).

After a knit stitch, before a purl stitch
Bring yarn forward between the needles, then back over the top of the right hand needle and forward between the needles again, so that it is now in position to purl the next stitch (Fig. 3c).

After a purl stitch, before a knit stitch
Take yarn over right hand needle to the back, so that it is now in position to knit the next stitch (Fig. 3d).

Fig. 3a

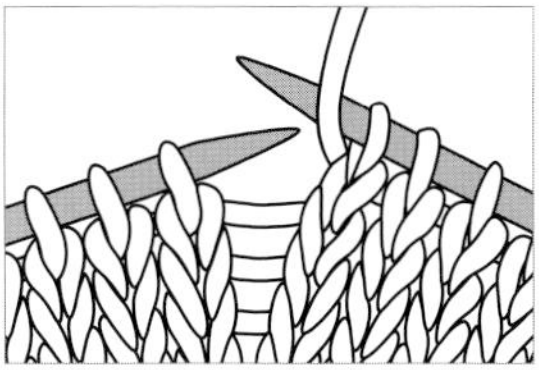

Fig. 3b

Fig. 3c

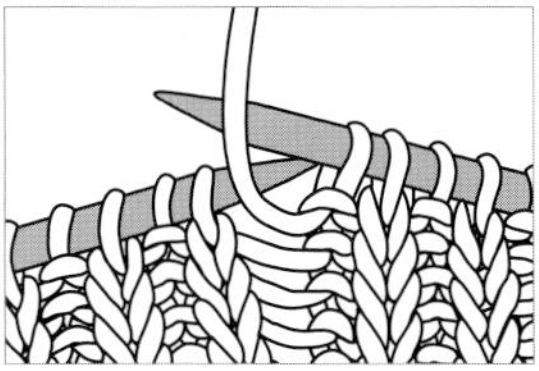

Fig. 3d

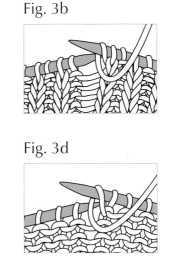

PICKING UP STITCHES

When instructed to pick up stitches, insert the needle from the front to the back under two strands at the edge of the worked piece (Figs. 4a & b). Put the yarn around the needle as if to knit, then bring the needle with the yarn back through the stitch to the right side, resulting in a stitch on the needle.

Repeat this along the edge, picking up the required number of stitches.

A crochet hook may be helpful to pull yarn through.

Fig. 4a

Fig. 4b

KNITTING NEEDLES		
UNITED STATES	ENGLISH U.K.	METRIC (mm)
0	13	2
1	12	2.25
2	11	2.75
3	10	3.25
4	9	3.5
5	8	3.75
6	7	4
7	6	4.5
8	5	5
9	4	5.5
10	3	6
10½	2	6.5
11	1	8
13	00	9
15	000	10
17	---	12.75

CROCHET HOOKS	
UNITED STATES	METRIC (mm)
B-1	2.25
C-2	2.75
D-3	3.25
E-4	3.5
F-5	3.75
G-6	4
H-8	5
I-9	5.5
J-10	6
K-10½	6.5
N	9
P	10
Q	15